Father Koala's Fables

Kel Richards

illustrated by Glen Singleton

ASHTON SCHOLASTIC
SYDNEY AUCKLAND NEW YORK TORONTO LONDON

For Shane and Sarah—KR

To Luke.
What a joy. This book and your birth all at the same time—GS

Richards, Kel, 1946–.
  Father Koala's fables.

  ISBN 1 86388 213 8.
  ISBN 1 86388 214 6 (pbk.)

  1. Fables, Australian. I. Singleton, Glen. II. Title.

398.2

Text copyright © Kel Richards, 1993.
Illustrations copyright © Glen Singleton, 1993.

First published in 1993 by Ashton Scholastic Pty Limited A.C.N. 000 614 577,
PO Box 579, Gosford 2250. Also in Brisbane, Melbourne, Adelaide, Perth and
Auckland, NZ.

The illustrations in this book were executed in ink and watercolour wash.

Typeset by David Lake Typesetting, Forresters Beach NSW.
Printed in Hong Kong.

12 11 10 9 8 7 6 5 4 3 2 1   3 4 5 6 / 9

Contents

Father Koala tells a tale

Father Koala settled back,
Sipping his billy tea.
He stared at the moon in the evening sky,
And here's what he said to me:

'Did I ever tell you the awful truth,
When the evening light was pale?
Did I ever tell you the awful truth,
That I have got . . . a tale?'

'A tail? Why, no! That cannot be!'
All of us started to shout.
'If koalas were creatures that all had tails,
You'd see them waving about!'

'I have a tale,' said Father Koala,
Just as he'd said before.
'In fact, I have two, or three, or six,
Or possibly even more!

'But these are not tails to wave about,
To beat away the flies.
These are tales to tell to others,
While the camp fire flickers and dies.

'So, young koalas, gather about,
Eat an apple or pear or peach,
And listen to all of the tales that I tell,
And learn the lessons they teach!'

5

The emu and the wombat

One day Emu was boasting of his speed to all the other animals in the bush.

'I have never yet been beaten,' he said. 'When I stretch my legs and run at full speed, why, I can even run the pants off a kangaroo! I challenge anyone here to race with me.'

One fat, waddling wombat said quietly, 'I will accept your challenge.'

'What a joke! What a joke!' hooted Emu with howls of laughter. 'I could beat you at half speed! I could dance around you like a brolga all the afternoon and still beat you! What do I care for a waddling wombat, when I can run the pants off a kangaroo?'

But the wombat was not interested in a boasting contest, and said simply, 'Shall we race?'

A course for the race was mapped out—from Gulargambone to Oodnadatta, then back again to Coolangatta.

The starter's gun was fired, and they were off!

Emu started at a sprint and had soon disappeared down the track in a cloud of dust. Wombat waddled away after him.

6

Before long, Emu was so far ahead he decided that he could safely lie down in the shade of a leafy wattle tree and have a little sleep.

Meanwhile, Wombat plodded on and plodded on, waddling along in a very wombatty sort of way. Emu opened one eye when Wombat passed. He murmured sleepily, 'Plenty of time to catch up and win the race later—much later.'

Emu then went back to sleep again.

Still Wombat wearily plodded on and plodded on in the blazing heat of the sun.

As Wombat was nearing the finish line, Emu decided it was time to wake up, start running, and win the race. So he stood up, stretched out his long, long legs, and took off like a tropical cyclone.

As Emu flashed towards the finish line, Wombat—slow, fat, waddling Wombat—stepped across the line and was declared the winner.

Moral: keep going quietly at your own pace,
slow and steady wins the race.

OODNADATTA

COOLANGATTA

The crow and the bandicoot

A big black crow was flying through the blue skies above the saltbush plain, when he saw the smoke of a swaggie's camp fire.

Swooping down to investigate, the crow was delighted to see that the swaggie had just cooked some fresh, hot damper. 'Ark! Ark!' said the crow hungrily as his tummy rumbled.

And while the swaggie was looking the other way, the crow swooped down, stole the damper, and flew away.

He came to rest in a small gum tree on the banks of a distant creek. At the foot of the tree was a burrow, out of which wandered a sleepy long-nosed bandicoot, curious to see what all the fuss was about.

For a moment the crow stared at the bandicoot, and the bandicoot stared at the crow with the piece of fresh, hot damper in his beak.

8

Then the very clever bandicoot said, 'How delighted I am to finally meet you, Mr Crow, for I have heard wonderful things about you. They tell me you have the sweetest voice in all the bush—more beautiful than the lyrebird, sharper than the whipbird and prettier than the bellbird. Oh, won't you please sing for me, Mr Crow?'

The crow puffed out his chest in pride and loudly cried, 'Ark! Ark!'

But the moment he opened his beak the damper dropped to the ground, where the bandicoot quickly grabbed it and hurried into her burrow. As she disappeared, her voice could be heard saying, 'That's enough of the concert, Mr Crow, I have all that I want now, thank you very much!'

Moral: never be fooled by folk who flatter you!

9

The goanna and the water buffalo

It was up in the gulf country on a very hot day, a long time ago, when a goanna happened to fall into a deep waterhole. It was a very dry, sandy waterhole, with just a trickle of water at the bottom.

She tried to climb back out again, but the sides of the hole were too steep and too high.

Late in the afternoon a big, black water buffalo passed by, and asked the goanna what she was doing at the bottom of such a deep waterhole.

'Oh, haven't you heard?' said the goanna, 'there is going to be a great drought, and I jumped down here so as to be close to the water when the drought comes. Why don't you come down, too?'

The water buffalo was impressed by this advice, and clambered clumsily down into the waterhole.

The goanna quickly jumped on his back, put her foot on his long horns, and jumped out of the waterhole.

Now the water buffalo was trapped down at the bottom of the hole and the goanna was safely out.

Moral: don't take advice from someone caught in a mess of their own making.

The kangaroo and the possum

A big red kangaroo was lying in the shade of a pepper tree trying to sleep, but every time he dozed off a little pygmy possum, scampering among the leaves, would wake him up.

The kangaroo stretched out one large paw and grabbed the possum.

'I think I should crush you under my big hind feet as punishment for disturbing my sleep, little possum!' he growled.

'Oh, please,' squeaked the pygmy possum, 'if you forgive me this time I shall never forget it. And, who knows, perhaps I might be able to do you a good turn one of these days!'

The kangaroo laughed out loud at the thought of the little possum ever doing him a good turn. But he was so amused that he let the possum go, and it quickly scurried back to the safety of a tall gum tree.

12

Some time later, the big red kangaroo was eating the fresh green leaves beside a riverbank, when he became caught in an old fishing net left behind by careless fishermen. The more he struggled, the more tangled he became until, at last, he could hardly move at all.

This is the end, thought the kangaroo to himself as he lay there. *I can't move. I can't feed myself. I'll just lie here until I starve to death.*

At that moment, who should appear from the bush but the little pygmy possum.

'I see you are in trouble,' she said. 'Perhaps I can help?'

And with the two long teeth in her lower jaw she nibbled through strand after strand of the net until the kangaroo was free.

Before he hopped away, the kangaroo bent down and shook her tiny hand.

'I am very proud,' he said, 'to have you as my friend.'

Moral: even little friends may be a big help.

The frill-necked lizard and the honeybee

During the wet season in the gulf country, a frill-necked lizard was lying on a log enjoying the warm sun and the cool breeze.

A honeybee went buzzing by, carrying a heavy load of nectar back to the hive.

'Why don't you stop and chat with me?' said the lizard, 'instead of all this buzz, buzz, buzz, and work, work, work.'

'But the work must be done,' said the bee. 'We are storing up honey for the dry season when there will be no nectar to gather. Why don't you do the same?'

'What a lot of bother!' sneered the frill-necked lizard. 'Look around you! There is plenty of food. Eat! Play! Enjoy yourself!'

But the honeybee went buzzing on her way, shaking her head sadly at such foolishness.

In time, the wet season came to an end and the grass and bush turned dry and brown. Food was scarce and the lizard began to feel hungry.

14

As the dry season continued, a very thin, very hungry, very thirsty frill-necked lizard came and knocked on the trunk of the hollow ghost gum where the bees lived in their hive.

'You knocked?' asked the honeybee who came buzzing out in response.

'Yes, I knocked,' croaked the lizard. 'Could you please spare a little honey for a very thin, very hungry, very thirsty frill-necked lizard?'

The bee flew back inside and asked the queen. 'Yes,' she replied. 'As long as the lizard agrees to never eat another of my bees.'

The lizard quickly agreed, and every day until the end of the dry season the bees would bring the frill-necked lizard a little honey to eat.

And when the wet season returned, with its lush grasses and harvest of fruit, it was greeted by a very different frill-necked lizard—a very polite, hard-working frill-necked lizard.

Moral: do the work that you can do, to help yourself and others too.

The bushranger and the blue cattle dog

Back in the days of the gold rush, a bushranger crept into the tent of a sleeping digger and stole the digger's gold nuggets—nuggets as big as chook eggs!

The bushranger shoved the nuggets into his coat pockets and jumped into the wide, swiftly flowing river to escape. When he reached the middle, where the river was deepest, he found the weight of the nuggets pulled him down—and he couldn't swim!

A blue cattle dog happened to be swimming across the river at the same time.

'Are you in trouble?' asked the blue cattle dog, as the bushranger splashed and thrashed about.

'No (gurgle, gurgle), I'm all right (bubble, bubble),' lied the bushranger.

'Are you sure?' said the blue cattle dog.

'Quite all right (bubble, bubble), thank you (gurgle, gurgle),' lied the bushranger as he went down for the second time.

'Because you do look as though you're drowning,' said the cattle dog.

The only reply was a loud bubble from underwater. When the bushranger's head finally broke the surface again he at last admitted, 'I'm drowning! Help me!'

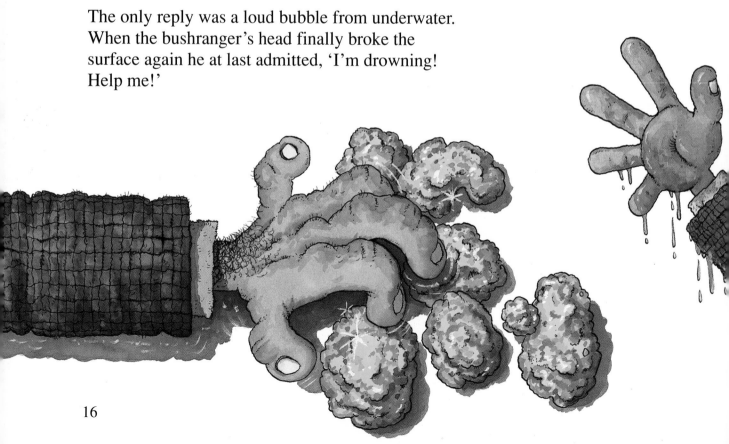

The blue cattle dog took hold of the bushranger's coat collar and began to pull him towards the shore. But before he had gone very far, the cattle dog stopped and said, 'You are far too heavy. Unless you take off your coat I cannot save you.'

So the bushranger took off his coat with the pockets full of gold nuggets. It promptly sank, to the bottom of the river.

The blue cattle dog then took him by the shirt collar and easily pulled the bushranger safely to shore.

Moral: dishonestly won wealth will weigh you down.

The cane toad and the bullock

'Oh, father,' said the little cane toad, sitting beside a dusty Queensland road, 'I have just seen a terrible monster! It was as big as a mountain, and it had horns on its head, and a long, long tail!'

'Don't be frightened, my son,' said the big old cane toad. 'That is only the old bullock who works for Ted the bullocky. And he isn't all that big.'

'Oh, yes he is, father! He is big. He is gigantic. He is ENOOOORMOUS!'

'Well, I admit he is tall my son, but I can make myself just as fat as he is.'

And so saying, the old cane toad huffed and puffed and blew himself up as big as he could.

'Oh, he is much bigger than that!' said the young cane toad.

The old cane toad puffed out his cheeks, and stuck out his chest, and blew himself up even bigger.

'Is he bigger than this?' he asked.

'Oh, bigger, father, bigger,' was the reply.

So the old cane toad took another deep breath and puffed and puffed, and swelled and swelled, and puffed and puffed, and swelled and swelled, until at last he went . . . POP!

He hissed like a popped balloon and ended up as flat as a leaf on the road.

Moral: if you burst with pride, you might end up looking very small.

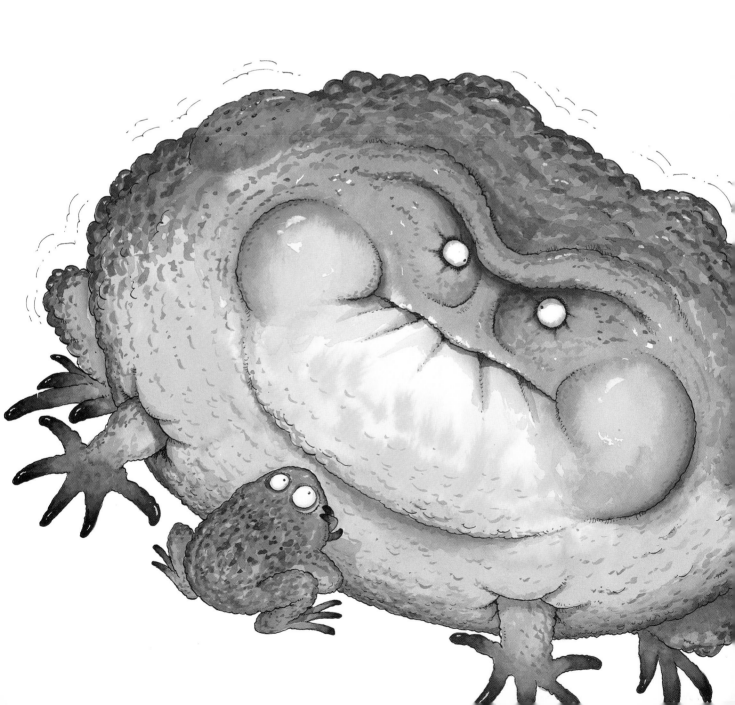

In the chook yard

In the darkness, just before dawn, a dingo crept
into the chook yard behind the homestead, looking
for a delicious chicken breakfast.

What a disappointment to find all the hens in the
henhouse, out of reach and safe from his fangs.

The dingo was about to leave, with his stomach
still empty, when a big red rooster fluttered down
from his perch, and strutted into the middle of the
chook yard. The rooster threw back his head and
loudly sang: 'Cock-a-doodle-DOOOO!'

Ah! thought the dingo, *I'll have my breakfast after all!*

The rooster, however, was not easy to catch. He
kept a sharp eye on the dingo, and every time those
sharp fangs began to move in his direction he
fluttered a safe distance away.

And so the dingo stalked warily around the chook yard. Once again the rooster crowed loudly: 'Cock-a-doodle-DOOOO!'

'What a fine voice you have, dear rooster,' said the dingo. 'Mind you, I once knew a rooster at Gundagai who had an even finer voice. He said the secret was to close his eyes while he crowed.'

The rooster, determined not to be second best, crowed again—this time with his eyes closed.

And in that instant, the dingo leapt upon him and grabbed him around the neck. The dingo held the spluttering rooster firmly in his jaws and ran out of the chook yard and back towards his home in the hills.

On the way he met another dingo, who greedily said, 'Caught a rooster have you? How about sharing half with me?'

'Tell him that you won't share me,' squawked the rooster. 'Tell him that I'm all yours.'

Yes, thought the dingo. *I will!*

But the minute the dingo opened his mouth to say these words, the rooster fell out of his jaws, spread his wings, and fluttered away to freedom.

Moral: never open your mouth when you should remain silent, and never close your eyes when you should keep watch!

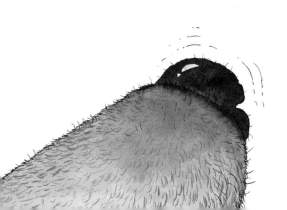

21

Andy O'Cleary

Many years ago, in the penal colony of New South Wales, a convict named Andy O'Cleary escaped from his guards and fled into the bush.

While wandering about, he came upon a large kangaroo lying down in the grass, moaning and groaning.

As he came near, the kangaroo held up one of his powerful hind feet which was horribly red and swollen. Andy looked closely and found that a large thorn, deeply embedded in the paw, was causing all the pain.

He carefully pulled out the thorn and bandaged up the paw of the kangaroo, who was soon up on his feet licking Andy's hand just like a grateful puppy.

Andy and the kangaroo became the best of mates. But at length, both Andy and the kangaroo were captured by troopers and taken in chains back to Sydney Cove. Andy was locked up in a cell, while the kangaroo was taught to box against humans and treated cruelly by the troopers.

On the next half holiday, a sporting carnival was held for the Governor and all his senior officers. Andy was dragged out of his cell and told that, to amuse the crowd, he was to fight a savage boxing kangaroo—whose giant hind feet could kill a man with a single blow.

Andy was terrified. But as soon as he came near the kangaroo he recognised his friend. And the kangaroo, instead of fighting, hopped over and began licking Andy like a happy puppy.

The Governor was amazed by this display and summoned Andy, who told him the whole story. As a reward, Andy was given a free pardon and the kangaroo was set free to return to the western plains that he loved.

Moral: making friends and doing good deeds, is like ploughing fields and sowing seeds—it leads to a harvest of happiness.

The boy who cried 'Bushfire'

There once was a young boundary rider—little more than a boy—whose job it was to look after the distant fences, a long way from the homestead.

It was rather lonely in those outlying paddocks, so he thought of a plan by which he could get a little company and enjoy some excitement.

He rode as hard as he could towards the homestead calling out, 'Bushfire! Bushfire!'

The squatter, and the squatter's wife, and all the stockmen, came rushing out to meet him, asking, 'What's the matter?'

When he told them he was only joking, some of them laughed nervously, some walked away in disgust, and some stopped to talk to him.

The young boundary rider enjoyed being the centre of attention so much, that a few days later he tried the same trick again. And again everyone rushed to his aid, only to find that he was playing another joke.

Shortly after this, there was a storm, and lightning struck the stump of a dead tree out on the farthest edge of the run. The tree burst into flames and the fire quickly spread to the dry grass and spinifex. Soon the whole paddock was ablaze.

Of course, the young boundary rider rode as hard as he could back to the homestead, shouting, 'Bushfire! Bushfire!'

But this time no one came running.

'You've fooled us twice, you won't fool us again,' said the stockmen.

'We've had enough of your lies,' said the squatter. 'Get back to work!'

Before the bushfire finally burnt itself out, it had destroyed all of the western sheds and fences on the property. When he found out what had happened, the squatter made the young boundary rider pay for the damage out of his own wages.

Moral: a liar ends up paying the price, they'll be believed just once or twice.

The kelpie and the dingo

A young kelpie pup lived in the homestead yard of an outback cattle station.

Every night, when the sun went down and the moon came out, the eerie howling of a dingo could be heard in the distant hills.

When this happened, the kelpie pup liked to sit on the veranda and yap back at the howling dingo.

'I'm as tough as you are,' he would yap. 'In fact, I'm tougher than you! I'll take on any dingo.'

Late into the night the dingo would howl and the kelpie would yap, until the kelpie's master would throw an old boot and shout out 'Stop that yapping!'

And this happened every night. Until, that is, one night, when the moon and the stars were hidden behind the clouds. In the darkness of that night there was an even blacker darkness creeping about. The kelpie could sense the black shape as it scratched and dug and slithered its way under the homestead fence.

And before he knew it, the slinking shape that was darker than night was standing before him on the veranda.

'Are you the kelpie who has been challenging me?' hissed the black shape, showing its yellow fangs as it spoke.

'What? Who? Me?' was all the kelpie could say, and it sounded like a whimper.

'I've come to take up your challenge,' hissed the dingo.

The next morning, when the kelpie pup limped back home, scratched and sore, battered and bruised, he knew that he had been in a fight.

Moral: if you boast and brag of what you can do, trouble will come looking for you.

The kookaburra and the billabong

One day a kookaburra was flying home, carrying a fat, juicy snake in her beak. She was planning to eat her slippery catch for dinner.

On her way home, the kookaburra stopped to rest in the branches of a gum tree that stood beside a billabong.

Looking down from the branch, the kookaburra saw in the water another kookaburra—and she, too, was carrying in her beak a fat, juicy snake!

The greedy bird on the gum tree branch wanted that snake too! So she opened her beak and cackled loudly, 'Give me your snake!'

But the moment she spoke, the snake fell out of her own beak and plopped into the water of the billabong.

Moral: be satisfied with what you've got—greedy folk can lose the lot!

28

The coming of the flood

On the banks of the Warrego River, downstream from Cunnamulla, lived a self-satisfied old platypus. One sunny afternoon he was lying in the grass, enjoying the breeze, when a flock of currawongs flew overhead, calling out a warning:

'Flood coming! Flood coming!' they cried. 'Higher ground! Move to higher ground!'

I don't need to move to higher ground, thought Platypus to himself. *Platypuses are different. I am just as much at home in the water as I am in my snug little burrow in the bank. Let the flood come, I have nothing to fear.*

By the time the sun was setting, the water in the Warrego had risen so far that Platypus had to leave his burrow and take shelter on a tall rock beside the rushing river.

29

Later that night, by the light of a bright yellow moon, Platypus saw a raft drifting down the flooded stream. On board were Koala, Wombat and Wallaby.

'Hop on board!' they shouted. 'Come with us further down the river. Once we reach the hills we will be safe from the flood.'

'Thank you, but I don't think I'll bother,' replied Platypus. 'I'm fine where I am. Platypuses are different. I'm a fine swimmer, and a flood doesn't frighten me.'

Try as they might, they could not persuade Platypus to join them and so, at length, they had to continue their escape without him.

As the night wore on, the floodwaters became higher and rougher, and Platypus found that his rock had become a tiny island surrounded by a sea of muddy, surging currents.

All night the water rose and roared.

And then, just before dawn, Platypus was swept off his rock by a wave of rushing water.

The muddy, flooded, wild waters pushed him this way and that. The currents hammered him against the bottom of the river, and then battered him against the tops of the trees, for the water had risen to great heights.

Platypus tried to swim against the current, but the water was full of broken fenceposts and tree branches that kept knocking him about. And the swirling, gurgling water was just so swift and